My Emotions
Emosyon Mwen Yo

ANGRY
FACHE

A Crabtree Roots Book
Yon Liv Crabtree Rasin

AMY CULLIFORD
JEAN-PIERRE GASTON

Crabtree Publishing
crabtreebooks.com

School-to-Home Support for Caregivers and Teachers

This book helps children grow by letting them practice reading. Here are a few guiding questions to help the reader with building his or her comprehension skills. Possible answers appear here in red.

Before Reading:

- What do I think this book is about?
  - *This book is about feeling angry.*
  - *This book is about what feeling angry looks or feels like.*

- What do I want to learn about this topic?
  - *I want to learn what to do if I feel angry.*
  - *I want to learn what feeling angry looks like.*

During Reading:

- I wonder why...
  - *I wonder why we yell when we are angry.*
  - *I wonder why we frown when we are angry.*

- What have I learned so far?
  - *I have learned that angry is an emotion.*
  - *I have learned drawing can help when you are angry.*

After Reading:

- What details did I learn about this topic?
  - *I have learned that it is okay to be angry.*
  - *I have learned that there are many ways you can cool down after being angry.*

- Read the book again and look for the vocabulary words.
  - *I see the word* ***vegetables*** *on page 4 and the word* ***yell*** *on page 7. The other vocabulary words are found on page 14.*

What makes me **angry**?

Kisa ki fè mwen **fache**?

I am angry when I eat **vegetables**.

Mwen fache lè mwen ap manje **legim**.

I **yell** when I am angry.

Mwen **rele** lè mwen fache.

I am angry when no one can play.

Mwen fache lè pesonn pa ka vin jwe.

I **frown** when I am angry.

Mwen **fronce sousi** lè mwen fache.

What can I do when I am angry?

Kisa mwen ka fè lè mwen fache?

I can **draw** a picture.

Mwen ka **desine** yon foto.

I can go ride my **bike**.

Mwen ka ale monte **bisiklèt** mwen an.

Words to Know
Mo pouw Konnen

angry
fache

bike
bisiklèt

draw
desine

frown
fronce
sousi

vegetables
legim

yell
rele

50 Words

What makes me **angry**?

I am angry when I eat **vegetables**.

I **yell** when I am angry.

I am angry when no one can play.

I **frown** when I am angry.

What can I do when I am angry?

I can **draw** a picture.

I can go ride my **bike**.

50 mo

Kisa ki fè mwen **fache**?

Mwen fache lè mwen ap manje **legim**.

Mwen **rele** lè mwen fache.

Mwen fache lè pesonn pa ka vin jwe.

Mwen **fronce sousi** lè mwen fache.

Kisa mwen ka fè lè mwen fache?

Mwen ka **desine** yon foto.

Mwen ka ale monte **bisiklèt** mwen an.

My Emotions

ANGRY

Emosyon Mwen Yo

FACHE

Crabtree Publishing

crabtreebooks.com 800-387-7650

Paperback 9781039624559
Ebook (pdf) 9781039625396
Epub 9781039624979

Printed in the U.S.A./CP102025

Library and Archives Canada Cataloguing in Publication
Available at the Library and Archives Canada

Library of Congress Cataloging-in-Publication Data
Available at the Library of Congress

Published in Canada
Crabtree Publishing
616 Welland Avenue
St. Catharines, Ontario
L2M 5V6

Published in the United States
Crabtree Publishing
347 Fifth Avenue
Suite 1402-145
New York, NY 10016

Written by: Amy Culliford
Designed by: Rhea Wallace
Series Development: James Earley
Proofreader: Ellen Rodger
Educational Consultant: Marie Lemke M.Ed.
Translator: Jean-Pierre Gaston
Production manager: Candice Campbell

Photographs: Shutterstock: Juan Pablo Gonzaález: cover; maxim ibragimov: p. 1; TY Lim: p. 3, 14; thevisualsyou need: p. 5, 14; wavebreakmedia: p. 6, 14; Olga Enger: p. 8-9, 14; Mandy Godbehear: p. 10; Julia Kuzhetsova: p. 11, 14; Spotmatik Ltd: p. 13, 14